World's Weirdest Plants

BRISTLECONE PINES ARE ANCIENT!

By Patricia Fletcher

Gareth Stevens
PUBLISHING

Please visit our website, www.garethstevens.com. For a free color catalog of all our high-quality books, call toll free 1-800-542-2595 or fax 1-877-542-2596.

Library of Congress Cataloging-in-Publication Data

Names: Fletcher, Patricia (Children's author)
Title: Bristlecone pines are ancient! / Patricia Fletcher.
Description: New York : Gareth Stevens Publishing, [2017] | Series: World's
  weirdest plants | Includes bibliographical references and index.
Identifiers: LCCN 2016029395| ISBN 9781482455991 (pbk. book) | ISBN
  9781482456004 (6 pack) | ISBN 9781482456011 (library bound book)
Subjects: LCSH: Great Basin bristlecone pine–Juvenile literature. | Rocky
  Mountain bristlecone pine–Juvenile literature. | Pine–Juvenile
  literature.
Classification: LCC QK494.5.P66 F625 2017 | DDC 585/.2–dc23
LC record available at https://lccn.loc.gov/2016029395

First Edition

Published in 2017 by
Gareth Stevens Publishing
111 East 14th Street, Suite 349
New York, NY 10003

Designer: Katelyn E. Reynolds
Editor: Kristen Nelson

Photo credits: Cover, p. 1 Paul Chesley/National Geographic/Getty Images; cover, pp. 1–24 (background) Conny Sjostrom/Shutterstock.com; cover, pp. 1–24 (sign elements) A Sk/Shutterstock.com; p. 5 Heather Lucia Snow/Shutterstock.com; p. 7 (map) Bardocz Peter/Shutterstock.com; p. 9 Dave Rock/Shutterstock.com; p. 11 Scott T. Smith/Corbis Documentary/Getty Images; p. 13 Dennis Flaherty/Science Source/Getty Images; p. 15 saraporn/Shutterstock.com; p. 17 Nagel Photography/Shutterstock.com; p. 19 W. Robert Moore/National Geographic/Getty Images; p. 21 (photo) Dieter Schaefer/Moment Open/Getty Images.

CONTENTS

Words in the glossary appear in **bold** type
the first time they are used in the text.

ANCIENT TREES

If you travel to the Rocky Mountains or southwestern United States, you may see odd-looking pine trees living at high **altitudes** with twisted trunks and very little bark. They're called bristlecone pines, and they may live for thousands of years!

There are two species, or kinds, of bristlecone pines. They both can live a very long time, but the Great Basin bristlecone pine is the longest-living **conifer** scientists know about. How have these trees been able to survive for so long?

This tree is over 1,000 years old!

MOUNTAIN HOME

Bristlecone pines commonly grow at altitudes between 6,500 and 11,000 feet (1,981 and 3,353 m). They're mostly found in the mountains of California, Nevada, and Utah. Great Basin National Park is home to many groves, or groups, of these trees.

The bristlecone pines' **habitat** is too **harsh** for many other living things to survive. They have **adapted** to living so high up. Unlike many other plants, they're able to grow in places with rocky soil, long winters, and little rain.

SEEDS OF KNOWLEDGE

There aren't a lot of bristlecone pines on Earth, and many are found in national parks where people can't harm them.

TWISTED TRUNKS

Bristlecone pine trees can have one or many trunks. The trunks often twist around one another, especially at higher altitudes. The trunks are light colored and smooth from the weathering of wind and rain.

Pine trees, including the bristlecone pine, are known for being needleleaf trees. The bristlecone pine's needles are yellow green. They're each about 1 inch (2.5 cm) long and grow in groups, or packets, of five. The needle packets completely cover each branch.

A bristlecone pine's needles can live 20 to 30 years on a branch!

9

GROW SLOW

Even though bristlecone pines are some of the oldest trees, they aren't the biggest. Most of a bristlecone pine's energy is spent surviving in its habitat, not growing.

At lower altitudes, bristlecone pines can grow to be 60 feet (18 m) tall. Those growing at higher altitudes are often only half that size! Bristlecone pines grow very slowly. A tree that's 40 years old may only be 6 inches (15 cm) high! It might grow less than 0.01 inch (.03 cm) in **circumference** each year.

SEEDS OF KNOWLEDGE

The amount of rain and other conditions play a big role in how much a bristlecone pine grows each year.

In Dixie National Forest in Utah, hikers can take the Twisted Forest Trail to see some old bristlecone pines.

CONES AND SEEDS

As conifers, bristlecone pine trees make seeds inside their pinecones. The bristlecone pine needs both male and female pinecones to do this. Each tree grows both. The male pinecones have pollen inside them. The pollen must reach the female pinecones and **fertilize** them. Wind commonly pollinates, or moves the pollen to, the female pinecones. Once fertilized, the female pinecones produce seeds.

Bristlecone pines can produce seeds for thousands of years! However, the older a tree gets, the fewer seeds it can produce.

Bristlecone pine trees' pinecones start out purple and then turn brown in about 2 years.

STAYING ALIVE

Bristlecone pines survive for so long for many reasons. First, in their habitat, there's no **competition** from other plants for **nutrients** in the soil or growth space. Their habitat also doesn't have lots of bugs or other living things that can be harmful to the trees.

The bristlecone pine has a lot of **resin** in its wood that plays a part in keeping pests away, too. The resin also keeps the trees from drying out.

SEEDS OF KNOWLEDGE

Bristlecone pines don't grow very close together. This way, if one catches fire, the fire won't harm others. In **denser** forests, fire can move quickly through many trees.

Bristlecone pines' slow growth makes their wood very dense, another way they keep pests and other problems away.

15

ENERGY SAVERS

Bristlecone pines are masters at saving energy for survival. Their needles live for many years, so the tree doesn't waste energy growing new needles.

In addition, bristlecone pines have a special root system. One big root feeds the part of the tree above it. When a root dies because it's been exposed, only the part of the tree right above it dies. When you see a bristlecone pine, much of it is dead already! The dried out, dead parts of the tree give its trunk its twisted look.

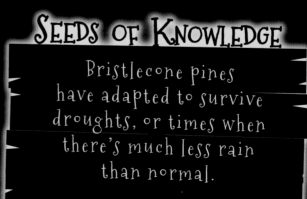

SEEDS OF KNOWLEDGE
Bristlecone pines have adapted to survive droughts, or times when there's much less rain than normal.

A bristlecone loses much of its bark after a drought, storm, or fire so there's less living matter to take care of.

HOW OLD?

Figuring out the age of most trees is as simple as counting the number of growth rings in their trunk. But with bristlecone pines, it's not always so simple. Some years, bristlecone pines don't grow, so no growth rings are added. Also, many are in state and national parks where they can't be cut down to study.

Sometimes, scientists are allowed to take out a pencil-sized piece from a living bristlecone pine to look at the growth rings. They also cut into dead bristlecone pines.

SEEDS OF KNOWLEDGE

Bristlecone pine trees' wood is so dense, the trees may stay standing for hundreds of years after they die!

In the 1960s, someone studying natural history was allowed to cut down a very old bristlecone pine named Prometheus. The tree turned out to be about 4,900 years old!

19

THE OLDEST

Hidden in the White Mountains of California lives the oldest bristlecone pine on Earth. It's more than 5,060 years old!

Another very old bristlecone pine grows in the White Mountains in the Ancient Bristlecone Pine Forest. It's named Methuselah, and you can visit it, but no sign says which tree it is! That's to stop people from harming the tree. Other trees in this forest are also thousands of years old, so you can still see history—and a very odd plant—growing right in front of you!

SEEDS OF KNOWLEDGE

Methuselah is said to be almost 5,000 years old!

FEATURES OF THE BRISTLECONE PINE TREE

> makes seeds with male and female pinecones
> grows many trunks that twist around each other
> grows needles in packets of five
> keeps little bark
> makes dense wood by growing slowly
> each part has its own root

GLOSSARY

adapt: to change to suit conditions

altitude: height above sea level

circumference: the length around the widest part of something

competition: the need by two or more living things for something beyond the supply

conifer: a tree that has evergreen, needlelike leaves and makes seeds in cones

dense: packed very closely together

fertilize: to add male cells to female cells to make seeds

habitat: the natural place where an animal or plant lives

harsh: hard to bear

nutrient: something a living thing needs to grow and stay alive

resin: a yellowish or brownish matter made in trees

FOR MORE INFORMATION

Books

Brucken, Kelli M. *Bristlecone Pines*. San Diego, CA: KidHaven Press, 2006.

Spilsbury, Louise. *Superstar Plants*. New York, NY: PowerKids Press, 2015.

Websites

Bristlecone Pines

nps.gov/grba/planyourvisit/identifying-bristlecone-pines.htm
Read more about bristlecone pines in Great Basin National Park.

Trees

ducksters.com/science/trees.php
Find out more about conifers and other kinds of trees.

INDEX